The Mayfl

M a r c   V

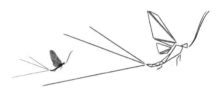

SPUYTEN DUYVIL

New York City

© 2024 Marc Vincenz

ISBN 978-1-963908-03-9

Cover and title page art: "The Mayfly" by Jake Quatt.
Book design, typography, and concept: Marc Vincenz and t thilleman.
Words, sonics and tonics: Marc Vincenz.

A smart **machine** will first consider
which is more worth its while:
to **perform** the given task or, instead,
to figure some way out of it.

for the Sans Serif

THE CODAS

More **Truths** Dancing into the Hereafter

The **All-Unseeing** Eye Moves behind the Curtain

Mechanical **Rats** Crystalizing

Fatal Wounds Liberated through Hearing

The Interrogatory **Reborn**

A **Common** Stew

Mysterious Blue **Eggs**

After a Sad Trickle of Water the **Ego** Enters the **Id**

With Broad Heart and Short **Memory**

More **Truths** Dancing
into the Hereafter

We danced through our magic garden,
planted as we pranced, seeded,
pollinated and then ran ahead **fertilizing**.

The Sun shone her illuminable rays.
The Rain wiled us in her wily ways.
From time to time we were guarded.

We devoted ourselves to the Will of the One.
In this way, we fashioned ourselves
a seat at the Custodians' table.

We never once contemplated our **actions**
would have consequences beyond the Will:
yet, sometimes there is a dichotomy

that simply can't be untangled no matter
how many IQ points have been assimilated,
as the Great Leader once said:

A specialist knows when to stop specializing:
in other words, it's not about the **background noise**,
but about a single note that rings true.

The **All-Unseeing** Eye
Moves behind the Curtain

We won't **observe** you, it was said.
Just you go on about your business, was said.
And so we watered our magic garden

in the **knowledge** that we were unseen.
Of course, that year, water was scarce,
the lakes and rivers and creeks bare and dry,

fish and beaver skeletons adorned the shores
in their ivory pleas; still the mayfly soared gracefully
above the bramble, prickly pears and rose thorns.

A glistening film clung on to the tree bark,
and the toadstools oozed and huffed and wheezed;
a solitary beaver attempted to build a bluff

upon a lonesome hill, where a few drops of dew
clung on to withered fronds of bamboo
still towering above the flaring rust of dawn.

Where there's the Will there's a rain, is said.
Anything you can **imagine** has happened, is said.
Today, on the other hand, is simply another day.

Mechanical **Rats** Crystalizing

When it all ran dry, we realized
water had to be reassigned by the Will of The One.
As such, we finally came to the conclusion

the only solution was to insert the mechanical rats.
Technology is a glass marvel, after all, it was said.
The man with the glass eye unsees you from here too, was said.

Glass, of course, was first created in a crafty desert.
The Phoenicians and their forebears had once spread **the word**:
from Cartagena to Corinth all and everyone **crystalized**.

The succulents gave themselves away, though.

The sand vipers slithered into their own **solitude**.

The mechanical rats became denizens of a desert nation.

They needed no water to survive, was said.

They felt no sentient **emotion**, was said.

They didn't breed like rabbits, was said.

And thus the rats became our new Custodians.

They cleaned every surface until it shone like silver, and

with surgical precision, they gleefully ate everything above the dirt.

Fatal Wounds
Liberated through Hearing

We dry-heaved, we coughed up soot.

We **injected** serums, infusions, root solutions.

In a manner of speaking, we found religion again.

The brass toilet seat upended seemed like a halo.

The paper roll, a **prayer** wheel often spun counterclockwise.

The words incanted like a psalm for the dearly departed.

We strayed our days in cafés along the boardwalk.

We painted towers and trestles and tetrahedrons.

We found light in the staccato and the **pulse** of the **hot** city.

We loved the night. We receded into the corners of our minds.
We reunited with fallen famers, dust-bowlers, dark-matter denouncers.
We had incontinence, premature ejaculation, excision, tattoos.

We needed nothing to **survive**, was said.
What about the nomenclature? was asked.
We don't breed like rabbits, was said.

We lived in the here-and-now, strove through
the theretofore, painted pictures like silver,
swirled, misted up, then rose back to the surface.

The Interrogatory **Reborn**

Whereas beneath the surface was what mattered.
Whereby the man with the glass eye unsees you from here too, is said.
Whereas the tidal forces aid in that predilection for pride.

There too, Mercury forces his point with a winged helmet
cast in the forges of **planetoids**, in the foundries of **solar systems**:
Here too, a human is a marvel too splendid to behold;

but beyond the cast-iron face, beyond the **funereal casket,**
the drink-until-you-still, the wise man raises his elbow
and forces those fungal spores to rise into the **Heliosphere**.

How a tidal force may be a station of **happiness**, or a slug,
devoid of all fiction, how a mercurial body may force their point
into all that breathes in this heady carbon dioxide.

Ethereal is what we called it, once upon the Blue Divide.
Sulfurial is what we **wished** it, once upon the Cardboard Wall.
And still, the mystery that we call the Great Unknown

has been spilled, foamy and **sanctified** by the One
in the word of the Common Spirit, that each and all shall devour
the warm words served up with pork dumplings and cabbage stew.

A **Common** Stew

And here too the gaze that caught so much:
the contemporaries and their small objects:
the polished-off antiques brought into **mainstream** view:

of the waffle or the snuffle we've come to suffer with too:
or so said Mother about her waifs; Father
was far too busy dredging his own liquid grave.

We all know those stories filled with disgrace
and disgust, whereby history tumbles about your ears:
memory is selective, **elective**, fills in cracks and **holes**.

Either way, the tide will carry you if you wish it or not:
the trolling waves ride up the last rocky outcrops:
the seabirds still hover here, grabbing and pulling and plucking,

seething in their own dewy, frothy brew—at least here
the **world** seems to appear for a second or two:
and still the **mystery** calls us back into the Great Unknown.

We broiled and basted for hours among the shitting pigeons and bats,
we sought out major viral **afflictions**, all for a historical panorama:
to watch that gorgeous flag raised up the ethereal flagpole.

Mysterious Blue **Eggs**

And when all the hens' eggs were devoured, some descended
upon the crags and cliffs, clinging to mossy outcrops: little hardy fowl
clasping the substrata hoping for a **drought** to pass over.

Here they forged and fenced their intentions, housed
into the lateral view squared away with their **pretensions**, usurped
and upended the all-held-belief, until, later, it became a life or a brief

hard to argue with: or so was said, or so someone once said:
Where there's the Will, there's the One, was once said.
Fork in hand: **Eat** not to be eaten, was also widely said.

Sharp protruding objects should be avoided, was clearly said.
Dead lead need not be burdened, was once said.
Lift yourself above the masses and puff out your chest, was said;

but above all, bring out those **beautiful** mysterious blue eggs.
Meanwhile, we prayed to the dead and dying hoping
they would send us maps of the Great Unknown

to guide our way into the Aftersurface:
They failed, and we ran amok, ran astray, ran away, upended.
Until once again the **heavens** descended.

After a Sad Trickle of Water
the **Ego** Enters the **Id**

Some said even mention of it was absolute heresy:
the Will of the One was not to be **cross-questioned**.
Just as the **language** of the Ancients was not to be **spoken**

by an other than the scientist in their eureka moments
on the rim of a golden toilet seat—or so the saying goes.
But then, what's said is truly never said, is also said.

Funny, how looking out into the distant valley
you might never recognize how many have gone
never to be seen again—least not here, on this side

of the Great Unknown where **eternal** enemies vie
for apex-predator status beneath the surface of **cyberspace**.
Doesn't biomimicry account for 97% of what we know? was once said.

Did we model ourselves upon the termites or the tigers? was asked.
Did we once worship them as we worshipped the One?
Even the scientists struggled to see deep into the Great Unknown.

But the Great Unknown glanced back, unrelenting, until,
one fine day, as the sun rose and feral creatures settled in their nests,
once again, the heavens ascended, or so has been told.

With Broad Heart
and Short **Memory**

She stripped the bark, and ate softly at the soft-fleshy under-bough,
right between the lines of storm years, when the mayflies—
every hundred years or so, seek out the most prolific pastures.

In these years they rise high into the lower thermals,
their thin-skinned wings at risk of tearing even in a minor gale:
But just who measures **wind or love**, my little mercies?

So says the unwitting Will of the One turning their Common Pages—
And yet they walked through the quick-shooting eucalyptus trees
looking for a mate to unburden their **conscience**—least, so said

the scientists, crossing their quickening hearts and hoping
we might crossbreed two gods into one, said one.
Another said, Even though her acorns may sleep in the shade,

a tree will always seek out the sun. Somewhere a voice
quietly nattering was pulling little levers in their cortex,
then said quietly: Isn't an acorn a tree in the **making**?

And, unseen, the Great Unknown cast their sharp eyes upon
an illegible script, something transcribed over a millennium ago,
once called the Vast Memory, now simply called **the Reward**.

The quotes at the beginning and the end of **The Mayfly Codex***, both emanate from the grand workings of Stanisław Herman Lem, a Polish writer of science fiction and essays on futurology, philosophy, and criticism, best known for his 1961 novel,* Solaris*.*

The Author

Marc Vincenz is a poet, fiction writer, translator, editor, musician and artist. He has published many books of poetry, fiction and translation. His more recent poetry collections, include, *The Pearl Diver of Irunmani*, *A Splash of Cave Paint*, *The King of Prussia is Drunk on Stars* and *Spells for the Wicked*.

Marc's work has been published in *The Nation, Ploughshares, Raritan, Colorado Review, Washington Square Review, Plume, Fourteen Hills, Willow Springs, World Literature Today, Golden Handcuffs Review, The Los Angeles Review of Books* and many other journals and periodicals.

His translation of Swiss poet Klaus Merz' selected poems, *An Audible Blue* won the 2023 Massachusetts Book Award for Translation. He is publisher and editor of MadHat Press and publisher of *New American Writing*, and lives on a farm in Western Massachusetts where there are more spiny-nosed voles, tufted grey-buckle hares and *Amoeba scintilla* than humans.

9 781963 908039